CONTENTS

Introduction

Welcome, Barbie fans! Thank you for your purchase!

It's so fun to crochet dolls' clothes, especially for Barbie. In this ebook you will find patterns to crochet Barbie outfit for every season. I added accessories for each outfit to complete the look, which also means you have a choice to mix and match. These crochet projects range from easy to intermediate skill level and you will learn or practice quite a few crochet stitches, depending on your crocheting experience. So grab your hook and yarn and let's have fun with crocheting new outfits for Barbie!

I recommend using cotton yarn for Barbie outfits because it won't stretch as much and it creates smooth look of the items, although other types of yarn work as well. I mainly use Patons Grace (weight 3), Alize Bella (weight 1) and Lion Brand Bonbons (weight 2), so weight category 1-3 is perfect.

Please refer to my video tutorials for visual illustration of stitches and techniques. You will conveniently find links to tutorials on 2nd page of each pattern.

All four Barbie outfits are original designs by HandmadebyRaine.

Please contact me with any questions or feedback about the patterns at handmadebyraine@gmail.com.

Thank you!

Happy crocheting!

Barbie Summer Outfit

Skill level	• Intermediate
Materials	• <u>Patons Grace cotton</u> (weight category 3) • 1 ball white (color A), 1 ball Aquifier (color B) - ball size 50g/1.75oz, 125m/136yds • Crochet hook 3.5 mm • Stitch marker • Button for backpack
Gauge	• 6 sc x 5 rows = 1 inch • 3 dc x 1 row • 4 hdc x 3 rows
Finished size	• Dress: 5 inches long on front, 4.25 inches around waist, 12.5 inches around skirt bottom edge • Backpack: 2.5 inches long, 2.5 inches wide • Sunhat: 7.5 inches around edge, 1.25 inches depth
Abbreviations – US terms	• ch = chain • sl st = slip stitch • sc = single crochet • blo = back loops only • dc = double crochet • hdc = half double crochet • beg = beginning
Special stitches	• Reverse sc = working from left to right (instead of usual direction) insert hook from front to back in next st to the right, yarn over, pull through the st, yarn over, pull through 2 loops on hook.
Video tutorials	• Dress https://youtu.be/ffjnfma-B4g • Backpack https://youtu.be/axZRooT1RA • Sunhat https://youtu.be/UdpuuZy_DbE

Instructions:

Barbie dress

- **Bodice:** with color A ch 26 and sl st in 1st ch to make a ring.

- Round 1 – sc in 1st ch, place stitch marker in that 1st sc, sc 1 in each ch (26 sc). Work in continuous rounds and move the marker up in 1st st on each round.

- Round 2 – sc blo in each sc (26 sc).

- Rounds 3-4 – repeat round 2.

- Round 5 – sc blo in each next 6 sc, skip 1 sc, sc blo in each next 12 sc, skip 1 sc, sc blo in each next 6 sc (24 sc).

- Round 6 – sc blo in each next 5 sc, skip 1 sc, sc blo in each next 12 sc, skip 1 sc, sc blo in each next 5 sc (22 sc).

- Round 7 – sc blo in each sc (22 sc).

- Rounds 8-10 – repeat round 7.

- Round 11 – sc blo in each next 5 sc, sc blo 2 in next sc, sc blo in each next 10 sc, sc blo 2 in next sc, sc blo in each next 5 sc (24 sc).

- Round 12 – sc blo in each next 6 sc, sc blo 2 in next sc, sc blo in each next 10 sc, sc blo 2 in next sc, sc blo in each next 6 sc (26 sc).

- **Skirt:**

- Round 13 – sl st in 1st sc, ch 2 (doesn't count as dc), dc blo in next sc, dc blo 2 in next sc, *dc blo in each next 2 sc, dc blo 2 in next sc = increase in every third st, repeat from*, end the round with 2 blo dc (34 dc), sl st in beg 2nd ch, don't cut the yarn.

- Round 14 – join color B with sl st and sc blo in each dc (34 sc), sl st in 1st sc, don't cut the yarn.

- Round 15 – join color A with sl st and repeat round 13 = increase in every 3rd sc (45 dc), sl st in beg 2nd ch.

- Round 16 – join color B with sl st and repeat round 14 (45 sc).

- Round 17 – join color A with sl st and repeat round 13 = increase in every 3rd sc (60 dc), sl st in beg 2nd ch.

- Round 18 – join color B and repeat round 14 (60 sc), fasten off and cut of the yarn.

- Round 19 – join color A with sl st and repeat row 13 = increase in every 3rd sc (77 dc), sl st in beg 2nd ch.

- Skirt edge – reverse sc blo in each sc, sl st in 1st sc, fasten off and cut off the yarn.

- **Shoulder straps:** join color A with sl st in 4th st from beg st on the back of the dress, sl st in 8 sc across the edge, ch 7 for shoulder strap, skip 5 sc and sl st in 8 sc across front edge of the dress, ch 7 for second strap, skip 5 sc, join with sl st in beg st.

- Sl st in upper loop of each sl st and each ch, sl st in beg st.

- Fasten off and weave in all ends.

Barbie backpack

- Round 1 – with color B make a magic ring and sc 8 in the ring. Place stitch marker in 1st sc, work in continuous rounds (three 1st rounds) and move the marker up in 1st st on each round.

- Round 2 - sc 2 in each sc (16 sc).

- Round 3 – *sc 1 in next sc, sc 2 in next sc, repeat from* (24 sc).

- Round 4 - *sc 1 in each next 2 sc, sc 2 in next sc, repeat from* (32 sc), sl st in beg sc.

- Round 5 - ch 1 and hdc in each sc (32 hdc), sl st in beg ch.

- Rounds 6 – 11 - repeat round 5.

- **String holes:**

- Round 12 - ch 1, *hdc 1 in each next 3 hdc, ch 1 and skip 1 hdc, repeat from* (8 string holes), sl st in beg hdc.

- Round 13 - sl st in each hdc and ch space, fasten off, cut off yarn.

- **Flap:** repeat rounds 1-3, then sl st in next 6 sc, (sc 1 in each next 2 sc, sc 2 in next sc) three times, ch 5 for buttonhole, (sc 1 in each next 2 sc, sc 2 in next sc) three times, sl st in 1st st, don't cut the yarn.

- Attach the flap onto bag with 7 sl st (starting in st on bag body before one of the string holes and ending in st after the next string hole) by inserting hook through next st on flap and 1st st on bag edge and pulling yarn through these stitches as well as working loop on hook, ch 6 for handle, sl st in beg space where the flap attaching started. Fasten off and cut the yarn.

- **Braided string:** with 1st color cut 3 strands, each 15 inches long, make a knot and braid the string, make a knot at the other end, it should measure appr. 8 inches from one knot to the other. Weave in the string through the holes of the bag.

- **Backpack straps:** attach color B with sl st in 1st hdc row on the backside bottom of bag where you want the 1st strap to start, ch 19, attach with sl st to hdc next to string hole under the handle (see photo below for stitch placement), sl st in each 19 ch and fasten off, cut off yarn (or don't cut off and sl st across the bottom of bag inserting hook in about 9 hdc on the beg hdc round as shown on the photo below), ch 19, attach with sl st to hdc next to the other string hole under the handle, sl st in each 19 ch and fasten off.

- Sew on the button, in space between 3rd and 4th row from the top.

- Weave in all ends.

Barbie sunhat

- Round 1 – with color A make a magic ring and sc 6 in the ring. Place stitch marker in 1st sc, work in continuous rounds and move the marker up in 1st st on each round.

- Round 2 – sc blo 2 in each sc (12 sc).

- Round 3 - *sc blo 1 in next sc, sc blo 2 in next sc, repeat from* (18 sc).

- Round 4 - *sc blo 1 in each next 2 sc, sc blo 2 in next sc, repeat from* (24 sc).

- Rounds 5-6 – sc blo in each sc (24 sc), don't cut off yarn.

- Round 7 – join color B with sl st and sc blo in each sc, sl st in first st, fasten off and cut off yarn.

- Round 8 – join color A with sl st, *sc blo 1 in next sc, sc blo 2 in next sc, repeat from* (36 sc).

- Round 9 – *sc blo 1 in each next 2 sc, sc blo 2 in next sc, repeat from* (48 sc), sl st in beg sc.

- Round 10 - sl st blo in each sc, sl st in beg st.

- Fasten off and weave in all ends.

Barbie Tunic and Shoulder Bag

Skill level	• Easy
Materials	• <u>Alize Bella</u> cotton (weight category 1) • 1 ball beige (color A), 1 ball dark pink (color B) – ball size 50g/1.76oz 180m/197yds • <u>Lion Brand Bonbon</u> cotton package Nature (weight category 2) • 1 ball cream (color C) – ball size 10g/28yds • Crochet hook 2.25 mm
Gauge	• Tunic: 5 hdc x 3 rows / 5 sc x 7 rows • Bag (not critical): 8 hdc x 3 rows
Finished size	• Tunic: 4 inches long on front, 4.5 inches around waist, 6.5 inches around bottom edge • Bag: 2.5 inches long, 3 inches wide
Abbreviations – US terms	• ch = chain • sl st = slip stitch • sc = single crochet • dc = double crochet • hdc = half double crochet • beg = beginning • sc2tog = single crochet 2 together • dc2tog = double crochet 2 together • blo = back loop only
Video tutorial	• https://youtu.be/aBvbkG706-I

Instructions:

Barbie tunic

- With color A ch 35, sl st in 1st ch to make a ring.

- Round 1 – ch 3 (counts as 1st dc here and throughout), dc 1 in each ch (35 dc), sl st in beg 3rd ch.

- Round 2 – ch 3, dc 1 in each dc, sl st in beg 3rd ch.

- Round 3 – ch 3, dc 1 in each next 4 dc, dc2tog, (dc 1 in each next 5 dc, dc2tog) four times (30 dc), sl st in beg 3rd ch.

- Round 4 – repeat round 2.

- Round 5 – ch 3, dc 1 in each next 3 dc, dc2tog, (dc 1 in each next 4 dc, dc2tog) four times (25 dc), sl st in beg 3rd ch.

- Round 6 – repeat round 2. Fasten off, don't cut off color A.

- Round 7 – join color B, make a slip knot, take hook out of knot loop and insert it through 3rd beg ch on previous round to pull slip knot through, ch 3 and dc 1 in each dc (25 dc), sl st in beg 3rd ch. Fasten off, cut off color B.

- Round 8 – continue with color A, pull it through 3rd beg ch on previous round, ch and sc in same space, sc 1 in each dc (25 sc), sl st in beg sc.

- Round 9 – ch 1 and sc in each sc blo (25 sc), sl st in beg sc.

- Rounds 10-17 – repeat round 9.

- Round 18 – ch 1 and sc in each next 5 sc blo, ch 8 for 1st sleeve hole, skip next 3 sc and sc in each next 9 sc blo, ch 8 for 2nd sleeve hole, skip next 3 sc and sc in each next 5 sc blo, sl st in beg sc.

- Round 19 – ch 2 (counts as 1st hdc), hdc in each sc (inserting hook through both loops) and ch (35 hdc), sl st in beg 2nd ch.

- Round 20 – ch 2, hdc in each hdc, sl st in beg 2nd ch, fasten off, cut off yarn.

- Weave in all ends.

Barbie shoulder bag

- With color B ch 4, sl st in 1st ch to make a ring.

- Round 1 – ch 3 (counts as 1st dc here and throughout), dc 2 in the ring, ch 2, (dc3 + ch2) three times, sl st in beg 3rd ch.

- Round 2 – sl st in next 2 dc and ch2-space, ch3 + dc1 + ch2 + dc2 in same ch2-space, (dc 1 in next dc, dc 2 in next dc, dc 1 in next dc, in next ch2-space dc2 + ch2 + dc2), three times, dc 1 in next dc, dc 2 in next dc, dc 1 in next dc, sl st in beg 3rd ch.

- Round 3 – sl st in next dc and ch2-space, ch3 + dc1 + ch2 + dc2 in same ch2-space, (dc 1 in each next 8 dc, in next ch2-space dc2 + ch2 + dc2) three times, dc 1 in each next 8 dc, sl st in beg 3rd ch.

- Round 4 – sl st in next dc and ch2-space, ch3 + dc1 + ch2 + dc2 in same ch2-space, (dc 1 in each next 4 dc, skip next 4 dc, dc 1 in each next 4 dc, in next 2ch-space dc2 + ch2 + dc2) three times, dc 1 in each next 4 dc, skip next 4 dc, dc 1 in each next 4 dc, sl st in beg 3rd ch.

- Rounds 5-6 – repeat round 4, fasten off, cut off color B.

- Round 7 – join color C = make a slip knot, take hook out of knot loop and insert it through ch2-space to pull slip knot through, in same ch2-space ch3

+ dc1 + ch2 + dc2, (dc 1 in each next 4 dc, skip next 4 dc, dc 1 in each next 4 dc, in next ch2-space dc2 + ch2 + dc2) three times, dc 1 in each next 4 dc, skip next 4 dc, dc 1 in each next 4 dc, sl st in beg 3rd ch.

- Round 8 – sl st in next dc and ch2-space, ch 1 and sc in same space, (sc 1 in each next 5 dc, sc2tog, sc 1 in each next 5 dc, sc 1 in next ch2-space, ch 25 for handle, sc 1 in next ch2-space) twice, instead of last sc (after 25 ch) just sl st in beg sc, fasten off, cut off color C.

- Weave in all ends.

- **Braided string**: cut 3 strands with color B, 10 inches each for belt and 3 strands, 15 inches each for hair piece. Braid and tie knots on both ends. Weave the belt string between dc stitches on round 7. Count 12 dc from the back (from beg of round) and insert string from front to back, skip 2 dc and using the hook pull the string from back to front, skip 2 dc, and repeat. You will have 3 dc between both string ends on the front.

Barbie Raincoat and Umbrella

Skill level	• Intermediate
Materials	• <u>Alize Bella</u> (weight category 1) • 1 ball yellow (color A), 1 ball light blue (color B) - ball size 50g/1.76oz 180m/197yds • Crochet hook 2.75 mm for raincoat • Crochet hook 1.5 mm to attach beads • Crochet hook 2.25 mm for umbrella • 4 glass beads size 2/0 or small buttons • 7.5-inch long wire for umbrella • stitch marker • tapestry needle
Gauge	• Raincoat: 7 hdc x 3 rows / 6 sc x 7 rows • Umbrella (not critical): 7 hdc x 3 rows
Finished size	• Raincoat: 5 inches long from shoulder to bottom, 7 inches around bottom edge • Umbrella: 13 inches circumference
Abbreviations – US terms	• ch = chain • hdc = half double crochet • blo = back loops only • sc = single crochet • sc2tog = single crochet 2 together • sl st = slip stitch • dc = double crochet • beg = beginning • fpdc = front post double crochet
Special stitches	• <u>fpdc</u> = yarn over, insert hook from front to back to front again around the post of next st, yarn over, pull the loop through st – 3 loops on hook, (yarn over and pull through 2 loops on hook) twice
Video tutorial	• Raincoat https://youtu.be/MaAg1PBSdbA • Umbrella https://youtu.be/Ts9TiLsCCcA

Instructions:

Barbie Raincoat

- **Main part**: with color A ch 22.

- Row 1 (wrong side) – ch 2 (don't count as 1st hdc here and throughout), hdc in 3rd ch from hook, hdc in each ch (22 hdc), turn.

- Row 2 (right side) – ch 2, hdc blo in each st (22 hdc), turn.

- Row 3 – ch 2, hdc in each st (22 hdc), turn.

- Rows 4 – 22 - repeat rows 2 and 3, don't cut off yarn.

- **Upper part**: turn the piece sideways facing right side.

- Row 1 – ch 1, sc 7 inserting hook in the side spaces of hdc rows (2 sc per each row), ch 8, skip 7 spaces, sc 16, ch 8, skip 7 spaces, sc 7, turn.

- Row 2 – ch 1, sc2tog in first 2 sc, sc 1 in each next 5 sc, sc 1 in each 8 ch, sc 1 in each next 16 sc, sc 1 in each 8 ch, sc 1 in each next 5 sc, sc2tog in last 2 sc (44 sc), turn.

- Row 3 – ch 1, sc 1 in each next 9 sc, sc2tog in next 2 sc, sc 1 in each next 22 sc, sc2tog in next 2 sc, sc 1 in each next 9 sc (42 sc), turn.

- Row 4 – ch 1, sc 1 in each next 9 sc, sc2tog in next 2 sc, sc 1 in each next 20 sc, sc2tog in next 2 sc, sc 1 in each next 9 sc (40 sc), turn.

- Row 5 – ch 1, sc 1 in each next 8 sc, sc2tog in next 2 sc, sc 1 in each next 20 sc, sc2tog in next 2 sc, sc 1 in each next 8 sc (38 sc), turn.

- Row 6 – ch 1, sc 1 in each next 7 sc, sc2tog in next 2 sc, sc 1 in each next 20 sc, sc2tog in next 2 sc, sc 1 in each next 7 sc (36 sc), turn.

- Row 7 – ch 1, sc 1 in each next 7 sc, sc2tog in next 2 sc, sc 1 in each next 18 sc, sc2tog in next 2 sc, sc 1 in each next 7 sc (34 sc), turn.

- Row 8 – ch 1, sc 1 in each next 6 sc, sc2tog in next 2 sc, sc 1 in each next 18 sc, sc2tog in next 2 sc, sc 1 in each next 6 sc (32 sc), turn.

- Row 9 – ch 1, sc 1 in each next 6 sc, sc2tog in next 2 sc, sc 1 in each next 16 sc, sc2tog in next 2 sc, sc 1 in each next 6 sc (30 sc), turn.

- Row 10 – ch 1, sc 1 in each next 5 sc, sc2tog in next 2 sc, sc 1 in each next 16 sc, sc2tog in next 2 sc, sc 1 in each next 5 sc (28 sc), turn.

- **Hood:**

- Row 1 (right side) – ch 1, sc2tog in first 2 sc, sc 1 in each next 11 sc, sc 2 in each next 2 sc, sc 1 in each next 11 sc, sc2tog in last 2 sc (28 sc), turn.

- Row 2 – ch 1, sc 1 in each 28 sc, turn.

- Rows 3 - 14 - repeat row 2, don't cut off yarn.

- Fold the piece inside out and holding upper edges of the hood together sl st in each st inserting hook through both sides, fasten off, cut off yarn.

- **Sleeves**: join color A with sc in one of the corners of sleeve holes on right side.

- Round 1 – sc 1 in each 8 ch loop, sc 1 in the corner space, sc 1 in each 7 spaces of hdc row on main part (17 sc), sl st in 1st sc.

- Round 2 – sc in next sc and insert stitch marker in that first sc, sc in each next 15 sc (16 sc). 1 sc got skipped when we started this round in the next sc (not first) on round 1.

- Rounds 3 – 15 - repeat round 2 in continuous rounds (no beginning or end), sl st in 1st sc, fasten off, cut off yarn.

- Join color B with sc in any sc on the sleeve, sc 1 in each sc, sl st in 1st sc.

- Sl st blo in each sc, after last sl st fasten off, cut off yarn.

- Repeat the same for the 2nd sleeve.

- **Edge & buttons:**

- **Bottom edge** – join color A on right side of work with sc in the side of 1st hdc row, sc 2 in the side space of each next hdc row (43 sc), fasten off, cut off yarn.

- **Front edge** – also working on right side:

- Row 1 – join color B with sc in left bottom edge sc row, sc 1 in each hdc of main part, sc 1 in side space of each sc row of upper part and hood, sc 1 between each beginning sc of main part, sc in right bottom edge sc row (94 sc), turn.

- Row 2 – ch 1, sc 1 in each sc, turn.

- Row 3 – sl st in each next 10 sc, (take the hook out of working loop, switch to finer hook and insert it through the bead first, then pull the working loop through the bead, switch back to bigger hook, sl st in each next 6 sc) three times, attach the 4th bead, sl st in each next sc until you have 29 sc left on opposite edge.

- **Buttonholes** – sl st in next sc, (ch 5, sl st in 5th ch from hook, sl st in each next 6 sc) three times, ch 5 and sl st in 5th ch from hook, sl st in each next 10 sc, fasten off, cut off yarn.

- Weave in all ends.

Barbie Umbrella

- With color B make a magic ring.

- Round 1 – sc 4 in the ring.

- Rounds 2-3 – sc 1 in each 4 sc - work in continuous rounds across the outer edge. Sl st in 1st sc.

- Round 4 – ch 3 (counts as 1st dc here and throughout), dc 2 in same space, dc 3 in each next 3 sc (12 dc), sl st in beg 3rd ch.

- Round 5 – ch 3, dc 3 in same space, finish the 4th dc by pulling through with color A. (Important: always keep the second yarn inside the stitches), fpdc around next dc on round 4, finish fpdc with color B, *dc 4 in next dc, finish the 4th dc with color A, fpdc around next dc on round 4, finish fpdc with color B, repeat from*, sl st in beg 3rd ch.

- Round 6 – ch 3, dc 1 in same space, dc 1 in each next 2 dc, dc 2 in next dc, finish the last dc with color A, fpdc around next dc, finish fpdc with color B, *dc 2 in next dc, dc 1 in each next 2 dc, dc 2 in next dc, finish the last dc with color A, fpdc around next dc, finish fpdc with color B, repeat from*, sl st in beg 3rd ch.

- Round 7 – ch 3, dc 1 in same space, dc 1 in each next 4 dc, dc 2 in next dc, finish the last dc with color A, fpdc around next dc, finish fpdc with color B, *dc 2 in next dc, dc 1 in each next 4 dc, dc 2 in next dc, finish the last dc with color A, fpdc around next dc, finish fpdc with color B, repeat from*, sl st in beg 3rd ch.

- Round 8 – ch 3, dc 1 in same space, dc 1 in each next 6 dc, dc 2 in next dc, finish the last dc with color A, fpdc around next dc, finish fpdc with color B, *dc 2 in next dc, dc 1 in each next 6 dc, dc 2 in next dc, finish the last dc with color A, fpdc around next dc, finish fpdc with color B, repeat from*, sl st in beg 3rd ch.

- Round 9 – ch 3, dc 1 in same space, dc 1 in each next 8 dc, dc 2 in next dc, finish the last dc with color A, fpdc around next dc, finish fpdc with color B, *dc 2 in next dc, dc 1 in each next 8 dc, dc 2 in next dc, finish the last dc with color A, fpdc around next dc, finish fpdc with color B, repeat from*, sl st in beg 3rd ch.

- Round 10 – ch 3, dc 1 in same space, dc 1 in each next 10 dc, dc 2 in next dc, finish the last dc with color A, fpdc around next dc, finish fpdc with color B, *dc 2 in next dc, dc 1 in each next 10 dc, dc 2 in next dc, finish the last dc with color A, fpdc around next dc, finish fpdc with color B, repeat from*, sl st in beg 3rd ch.

- Round 11 – ch 3, dc 1 in each next 13 dc, finish the last dc with color A, fpdc around next dc, finish fpdc with color B, *dc 1 in each next 14 dc, finish the last dc with color A, fpdc around next dc, finish fpdc with color B, repeat from*, DON'T change to color B on last fpdc, with color A sl st in beg 3rd ch, cut off color B.

- Round 12 – ch 1, *sc blo in each next dc, sc in fpdc, repeat from*, sl st in beg ch. Fasten off, cut off color A.

- Weave in all ends.

- Cut 6 strands of color B, each 7 inches long.

- Working on the inside of the umbrella and using tapestry needle insert each strand through the posts of 4 dc on round 5. Leave about the same length of tail on both sides to tie around the stick.

- Apply some glue on top of the umbrella stick, then insert it in umbrella nub.

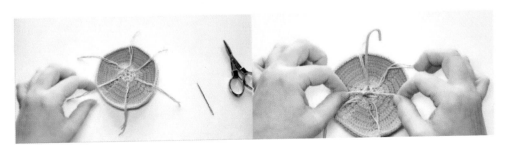

- Grab 2 pairs of strands on opposite sides, wrap the first pair around the stick, then wrap the opposite pair in opposite direction around the stick, so you can tie them in a knot around the stick. Make a double knot. Repeat three times and trim the ends.

Barbie Sweater and Hat

Skill level	• Easy
Materials	• <u>Alize Bella</u> (weight category 1) • 1 ball white (color A), 1 ball pink (color B) – ball size 50g/1.76oz 180m/197yds • Crochet hook 2.75 mm for sweater • Crochet hook 3 mm for hat • 1-inch pom pom • yarn needle
Gauge	• Sweater: 7 sc x 5 rows = 1 inch • Hat: 7 sl st x 10 rows = 1 inch
Finished size	• Sweater: 4.5 inches long from shoulder to bottom, 6.5 inches around bottom edge • Hat: 2 inches from top to botton, 4.5 inches around
Abbreviations – US terms	• ch = chain • sc = single crochet • flo = front loops only • sl st = slip stitch • blo = back loops only
Pattern notes	• The sweater is worked in one piece starting with 1ˢᵗ sleeve, then adding front and back panels and ending with 2ⁿᵈ sleeve. Front loop single crochet stitches create the vertical stripes of the sweater. The hat is also worked sideways with back loop slip stitch rows creating the stripes of hat.
Video tutorial	• Sweater https://youtu.be/EAaX5Le0FIA • Hat https://youtu.be/d6FZ0c0Z9LE

Instructions:

Barbie Sweater

- **1st sleeve:** with color A (leave longer tail for stitching later) ch 16.

- Row 1 – sc in 2nd ch from hook and in each ch (15 sc), ch 1 and turn.

- Rows 2-11 – sc flo in each st, ch 1 and turn.

- Row 12 – sc flo in each st, ch 20 for front panel.

- Row 13 – sc in 2nd ch from hook and in each ch (19 sc), sc flo in each 15 sc, ch 20 for back panel.

- Row 14 – sc in 2nd ch from hook and in each ch, sc flo in each next 34 sc (53 sc), ch 1 and turn.

- Rows 15-19 – sc flo in each sc (53 sc), ch 1 and turn.

- Rows 20-21 – sc flo in each next 21 sc, ch 1 and turn.

- Row 22 – sc flo in each next 21 sc, ch 11 for neck opening, skip 11 st, sc flo in each next 21 sc, ch 1 and turn.

- Row 23 – sc flo in each next 21 sc, sc in each 11 ch, sc flo in each next 21 sc (53 sc), ch 1 and turn.

- Rows 24-28 – sc flo in each sc (53 sc), ch 1 and turn.

- Row 29 – sc flo in each next 34 sc, ch 1 and turn. Front and back panels completed.

- **2nd sleeve:**

- Rows 30-41 – sc flo in each next 15 sc, ch 1 and turn.

- Leaving longer tail fasten off, cut off.

- Fold the piece in half to have sc flo rows running vertically.

- Using needle and long tails stitch the sides together and turn the piece right side out.

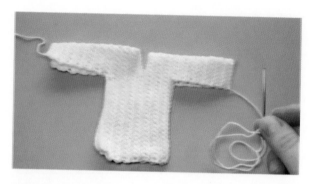

- **Bottom edge:**

- Join color A with sc in end of 1st sc row, sc in end of each row inserting hook in 2nd st from the edge, not the closest to edge (30 sc), sl st in 1st sc.

- Sl st in each sc around, sl st in 1st st, fasten off, cut off.

- **Neckline edge:**

- Join color B with sc in back opening (rows 20-21), sc in each st around neck opening inserting hook in 2nd st from the edge, not the closest to edge (32 sc), sl st in 1st sc, fasten off, cut off.

- **Sleeve edge:**

- Join color B with sl st in st by the sleeve seam, sl st in each st around. ATTENTION! before making the last sl st, cut off yarn, insert hook in same st where 1st sl st started and pull the yarn tail through the st and loop on hook.

- 3 little buttons on front are optional.

- Weave in all ends.

Barbie Hat

- With color A ch 12.

- Row 1 – sl st in 2nd ch from hook and in each ch (11 sl st), ch 1 and turn.

- Row 2 – sl st blo in each next 9 st (leave last 2 st unworked), ch 1 and turn.

- Row 3 – sl st blo in each next 9 st, ch 1 and turn.

- Row 4 – sl st blo in each next 9 st, sl st in each 2 unworked st on Row 1 (11 sl st), ch 1 and turn.

- Row 5 – sl st blo in each next 11 st, ch 1 and turn.

- Rows 6-37 – repeat rows 2-5.

- Row 38 – sl st blo in each next 11 st, ch 1 and turn.

- Fold the piece in half, sl st the sides together inserting hook through sl st on last row and foundation chains. Don't cut off.

- **Edge:**

- Turn the piece right side out, sc in every other end of row around bottom edge, inserting hook in 2nd st from the edge, not the closest 1st st – see the next photo, (19 sc), sl st in 1st sc.

- Sl st in each sc around, sl st in 1st st, fasten off, cut off.

- Using yarn needle stitch around the top edge and pull it tight, then stitch through the pom pom to attach it to the hat.

- Weave in all ends.

Printed in Great Britain
by Amazon

25243797R00018